Surviving the Forest

Pistol Horatiu

TABLE OF CONTENTS

Disclaimer

The information in this book is strictly for educational purposes. It is not intended as a substitute for professional advice, diagnosis, or treatment. The author and publisher of this book make no express or implied claims or guarantees regarding the book's completeness, accuracy, reliability, appropriateness, or availability for any purpose, or about the information, goods, services, or related graphics contained in the book. Any reliance on such information is entirely at your own risk. The author and publisher of this book accept no responsibility for any damages resulting from its use.

You acknowledge that you understand and agree to the terms of this disclaimer by reading and using the material in this book. When using any of the survival tactics taught in this book, it is your duty to exercise prudence and common sense. The author and publisher of this book are not responsible for any injuries or losses that may occur as a result of using the information included in this book.

This disclaimer is not meant to limit the author's or publisher's liability in any way. It is only offered to alert readers that the material contained in this book is supplied "as is" and is intended for educational purposes only. Use of the information contained in this book is at your own risk.

Surviving the Forest

Build a shelter`

If you are stranded in the woods overnight, you must have a dry, warm place to sleep. You can make a shelter using natural materials such as branches, leaves, and moss, or you can use a survival blanket, tarp, or other lightweight, portable materials.

Look for an appropriate location: Choose a place that is somewhat flat, dry, and away from any potential risks, such as steep slopes, bodies of water, or regions with heavy animal traffic.

Gather materials: Gather branches, leaves, grass, and other natural resources to utilize in the construction of your shelter. You should also bring a knife or other equipment to assist you in cutting and shaping the materials.

Build the frame: Use branches to create the basic frame of your shelter. Lean the branches at an angle against each other and connect them with vines, bark strips, or other flexible materials. Make sure the frame is robust and able to hold the weight of the materials you will be using to cover it.

Cover the frame: Cover the frame of your shelter with leaves, grass, or other natural materials. Make sure to overlap the layers and fill up any gaps to make a sturdy, waterproof cover. If available, you can also use a tarp or other waterproof material.

Cut a small aperture at the front of the shelter to serve as an entrance. To keep the wind and rain out, cover the aperture with a flap of material.

Make a bed: Gather soft, dry materials such as leaves, grass, and pine needles to create a comfortable bed inside your shelter.

Try out the shelter: Before settling in for the night, make sure your shelter is solid and adequate to shield you from the elements. If it seems unsteady or prone to leaks, make any required changes before settling in for the night.

Know how to make a shelter using a tarp or survival blanket.

Find an appropriate site for your shelter. This should be a dry, level place that is protected from the wind and rain. a way to go around it. a way to get around it. a way to get around it. a way to get around it.

Collect items to use as shelter supports. This might be anything from branches to sticks to rocks. You will need enough materials to make a frame for your shelter.

Using the materials you've acquired, construct the frame for your shelter. Arrange the elements in a rectangle or square form and secure them in place with a flexible vine or bark.

Cover the top of the frame with a tarp or survival blanket. Check that the tarp or blanket is large enough to cover the entire structure and is securely fastened in place with the flexible vine or bark.

Adjust the tarp or blanket to create an opening for the door. This can be accomplished by folding the tarp or blanket over itself to form a flap, or by simply cutting an opening in the material.

Use additional materials to produce insulation and additional protection from the weather, such as leaves or grass.

Test the stability and security of your shelter before using it. Make sure the frame is robust and that the tarp or blanket is securely in place.

It is crucial to note that building a shelter in the woods can be difficult and requires some basic survival knowledge. If you are stranded in the woods and do not feel confident in your capacity to build a shelter, your first goal should be to discover a method to get back to civilization or to locate aid.

Learn how to make a shelter using a tent.

Find an appropriate site for your shelter. This should be a dry, level place that is protected from the wind and rain. a way to go around it. a way to get around it. a way to get around it. a way to get around it.

Lay out the tent in the place you have picked. Ascertain that the tent is oriented in the direction that will provide the maximum wind and rain protection.

The term "electronic commerce" refers to the sale of electronic goods. Typically, this will entail attaching the poles to the tent and fastening the tent to the ground with the stakes provided.

Examine the tent for any signs of damage or wear, and repair or replace any damaged pieces as needed.

Once the tent is entirely erected, test its stability and security. Make sure the tent is robust and that all of the stakes are securely in place.

Store any gear or supplies inside the tent and seal the door to keep out any undesirable animals or insects.

It is crucial to note that using a tent to make a shelter in the bush requires some basic understanding of camping and survival skills. If you are lost in the forest and do not feel confident in your abilities to set up a tent, your first goal should be to find a method to get back to civilization or to locate aid.

Know how to make a shelter using natural materials.

Find an appropriate site for your shelter. This should be a dry, level place that is protected from the wind and rain. a way to go around it. a way to get around it. a way to get around it. a way to get around it.

Collect items to use as shelter supports. This might be anything from branches to sticks to rocks. You will need enough materials to make a frame for your shelter.

Using the materials you've acquired, construct the frame for your shelter. Arrange the elements in a rectangle or square form and secure them in place with a flexible vine or bark.

Locate materials for your shelter's roof. This could be anything from leaves to grass to bark. Place the materials on top of the frame and secure them with the flexible vine or bark.

Use additional materials to produce insulation and additional protection from the weather, such as leaves or grass.

Test the stability and security of your shelter before utilizing it. Make sure the frame is robust and that the roof materials are securely in place.

It is crucial to remember that creating a shelter out of natural resources can be difficult and requires some fundamental survival knowledge. If you are lost in the bush and do not feel confident in your capacity to build a shelter, your first goal should be to discover a way to get back to civilization or to locate aid.

Find and purify water.

Water that is clean and safe to drink is necessary for survival. Water can be found by searching for sources such as streams, rivers, and lakes, as well as by collecting precipitation. To remove pollutants or bacteria, it is critical to filter any water you gather before consuming it.

Look for sources of water: There are many potential sources of water in the forest, including streams, rivers, ponds, and lakes. Look for regions with damp ground or a higher concentration of flora, as these may suggest the existence of water. You might also look for animal footprints or other evidence of animal activity, as animals often need water and may guide you to a source.

Collect the water: Once you have found a source of water, you will need to collect it. You can use a container, such as a bottle or a canteen, to scoop up the water. If you do not have a container, you can use a piece of cloth or a piece of bark to collect the water and then wring it out into a container.

Purify the water: It is important to purify the water before drinking it to kill any potentially harmful bacteria or viruses. There are several methods you can use to purify water in the forest:

Boiling: Boiling water for at least 1 minute is an efficient approach to eliminating most germs and viruses.

Chemical treatment: You can use water purification tablets or drops to kill bacteria and viruses. Follow the instructions on the package for the proper dosage.

Filtration: You can use a water filter or a piece of cloth to filter out pollutants from the water.

To prevent contamination, it is critical to store the water in a clean container once it has been cleansed.

Start a fire.

A fire can give warmth, light, and a way to cook food. You can start a fire with a fire starter, matches, or fire-starting equipment such as flint and steel. Before starting the fire, gather dry tinder, kindling, and fuel.

Gather materials: To start a fire, you'll need a variety of things, including tinder, kindling, and fuel. Tinder is a flammable material, such as dry leaves, grass, or paper. Kindling is defined as little, dry twigs or branches that can be utilized to build a fire once it has been started. Those who want to Those who want to get in Those who want to get in

Find a suitable location. Choose a spot that is relatively flat, dry, and clear of any flammable materials. You will also need to find a way to contain the fire, such as by building a fire pit or using a stove or grill.

Make a fire lay: To begin, place a tiny amount of tinder in the centre of the chosen site. Then, on top of the tinder, add a layer of kindling, followed by a layer of fuel. Make sure the materials are arranged in a way that allows air to circulate, since this will help the fire burn more efficiently.

Using a fire starter: A fire starter is a tool that is designed to help you start a fire. Examples include matches, lighters, and ferro rods.

Using a fire bow: A fire bow is a tool that uses friction to create heat and start a fire. To use a fire bow, you will need a bow, a spindle, and a fireboard. Place the spindle in the centre of the fireboard and hold it in place with your foot. Then, use the bow to create a back-and-forth motion, applying pressure to the spindle as you go. This will create friction and heat, which will eventually cause the tinder to catch fire.

Using a fire lens: A fire lens is a tool for starting a fire that employs sunlight. You will need a lens to utilize a fire lens, such as a magnifying glass or a piece of clear plastic. Hold the lens above the tinder and direct sunlight at it until it catches fire.

Maintain the fire: Once the fire is started, you will need to maintain it by adding more fuel as needed. Keep a safe distance away from the fire and never leave it unattended.

Understand how to start a fire with a fire starter.

Gather materials for your fire. You will need tinder, kindling, and fuel. Tinder is a material that is easy to ignite, such as dry leaves, grass, or paper. Kindling is small, dry twigs or branches that will catch fire easily once the tinder is burning. Fuel is larger logs or branches that will provide sustained heat once the fire is established.

Find an appropriate spot for your fire. This should be a dry, flat place that is protected from the wind. Make sure you are not in an area where a fire could spread or cause harm.

Make room for your fire. Remove any leaves, grass, or other combustible debris from the area where you will be building your fire.

Make a fire ring or pit out of rocks or other materials to contain the fire and keep it from spreading.

Arrange the tinder, kindling, and fuel in a pyramid, starting with the tinder and ending with the kindling and fuel.

To light the tinder, use the fire starter. This could be a match, a lighter, or a fire starter such as a ferro rod.

Once the tinder has ignited, gently blow on the flames to help them spread to the kindling. As the kindling catches fire, add more kindling and fuel to the fire to keep it burning.

When starting a fire, it is critical to use caution. Make sure you have the right permissions and follow all local restrictions surrounding the use of fire. Keep an eye on the fire at all times and never leave it unattended.

Learn how to start a fire with friction.

If you need to start a fire with friction, follow these steps:

Gather supplies for your fire. A fireboard, a spindle, and a fireboard base are required. The term "electronic commerce" refers to the sale of electronic goods. The spindle should be a straight, dry piece of wood about the thickness of a pencil. A flat piece of wood or other sturdy surface should serve as the fireboard base.

Find an appropriate spot for your fire. This should be a dry, flat place that is protected from the wind. Make sure you are not in an area where a fire could spread or cause harm.

Make room for your fire. Remove any leaves, grass, or other combustible debris from the area where you will be building your fire.

Make a fire ring or pit out of rocks or other materials to contain the fire and keep it from spreading.

Set the fireboard on top of the fireboard base. The depression in the board's centre should be facing up.

Place a small amount of tinder, such as dry grass or leaves, in the depression in the centre of the fireboard.

With one hand, hold the spindle and insert the pointed end into the depression in the centre of the fireboard. Place the opposite end of the spindle on top of the fireboard.

Using a sawing motion, rub the spindle back and forth on the fireboard. This will generate heat and friction, causing the tinder to ignite.

Once the tinder has ignited, gently blow on the flames to help them spread to the kindling. As the kindling catches fire, add more kindling and fuel to the fire to keep it burning.

It is vital to remember that starting a fire with friction is difficult and takes practice and patience. It may take several attempts to ignite the fire, and your approach may need to be adjusted as you go. It is also necessary to use caution when lighting a fire. Make sure you have the right permissions and follow all local restrictions surrounding the use of fire. Keep an eye on the fire at all times and never leave it unattended.

Know how to make a fire using a solar still.

A solar still is a device that purifies water by using the heat of the sun. It is not a way to ignite a fire. You can start a fire with a fire starter, such as a match, lighter, or ferro rod, or you can use friction to build heat and ignite tinder.

A container, such as a large plastic bottle or a metal can, a piece of translucent plastic sheeting, and some rocks or other weights are required to build a solar still.

Locate an appropriate place for your solar still. This should be a well-lit area that is free of clutter and pollutants.

Place the container in the centre of the clear plastic covering.

Place the boulders or weights around the edges of the plastic sheeting to hold it in place.

Place a small cup or bowl in the centre of the container.

Pour water into the container with care, being careful not to spill any on the plastic sheeting.

Cover the container and plastic sheeting with a huge rock or other weight to keep everything in place.

Allow the water to evaporate and condense on the underside of the plastic sheeting as the sun heats it. The term "electronic commerce" refers to the sale of electronic goods.

It is crucial to realize that a solar water heater is not always a reliable source of drinking water and should not be relied on as the sole source of hydration. In a survival crisis, having numerous sources of water available is a smart idea.

Know how to make a fire using a fire piston.

A fire piston is a device that generates a spark by using a piston and compressed air to start a fire. Follow these steps to use a fire piston:

Gather materials: In addition to the fire piston, you will also need some tinder (such as dry grass, leaves, or bark shavings), a fire starter (such as dryer lint or char cloth), and some kindling (such as small sticks or twigs).

Prepare the tinder and fire starter: Make a small mound of tinder and fire starter on a level area.

Load the fire piston as follows: Remove the plunger from the fire piston and insert a small tinder piece into the chamber.

Compress the air: Hold the fire piston vertically and place the plunger back into the chamber. Quickly push the plunger down with vigoro to compress the air inside the chamber.

Ignite the tinder: The compressed air spark should ignite the tinder inside the chamber. If it does not, you may need to try again, using a new type of tinder or increasing the power with which you compress the air.

Transfer the flame to the kindling and tinder: Remove the ignited tinder from the fire piston and lay it on top of the kindling and tinder pile. To encourage the fire to expand, add kindling to the pile and gently blow on the tinder.

It may take some experience to get the hang of using a fire piston, but with patience and perseverance, you should be able to start a fire this way.

Understand how to light a fire with a lens.

A lens capable of focusing sunlight onto a small, concentrated point, as well as some tinder (such as dried grass, leaves, or bark shavings), a fire starter (such as dryer lint or char cloth), and some kindling are required to make a fire using a lens (such as small sticks or twigs). Follow these procedures to create a fire using a lens:

Gather materials: In addition to the lens, you will need some tinder, a fire starter, and some kindling.

Find a bright spot: Find a sunny area where you can direct sunlight onto your tent.

Prepare the tinder and the fire starter: Make a small amount of tinder and place the fire starter on a level area.

Concentrate the light: Place the lens in front of the sun and tilt it to focus the light on the torch. The lens should be close enough to the tinder, so the concentrated sunlight is hot enough to ignite it, but not so close that it scorches or burns it.

Light the tinder: The tinder should be ignited by the concentrated sunlight. If it doesn't, try again with a different type of igniter or by shifting the lens's angle.

Transfer the flame to the tinder and kindling: Once the tinder is lit, carefully add kindling to the pile and softly blow on the tinder to encourage the fire to develop.

It may take some effort to get the hang of starting a fire with a lens, but with time and determination, you should be able to do it. Just be careful while handling the lens and concentrated sunlight since they may get very hot and potentially deadly.

Know how to make a fire using a battery and steel wool.

A 9-volt battery, fine steel wool, and tinder are required to start a fire with a battery and steel wool (such as dry grass, leaves, or bark shavings). You'll also need kindling (small sticks or twigs) to help the fire develop once it's lit. To ignite a fire with a battery and steel wool, follow these steps:

Gather materials: You'll also need tinder and kindling in addition to the battery and steel wool.

Prepare the tinder and kindling as follows: Make a small mound of tinder and kindling on a flat surface.

Unroll the steel wool. Unroll a little bit of steel wool to make a thin, fluffy thread.

Touch the ends of the steel wool to the battery terminals: Place one end of the steel wool against the battery's positive terminal (typically labelled with a "+" symbol) and the other end against the negative terminal (usually marked with a "-" symbol). The steel wool should begin to light and spark at this point.

Transfer the sparks to the tinder as follows: Carefully move the flaming steel wool near the tinder and blow on it gently to encourage the sparks to leap to the tinder. The tinder should begin to melt and catch fire.

Once the tinder has been ignited, carefully add kindling to the pile and softly blow on the tinder to encourage the fire to develop.

It may take some effort to get the hang of lighting a fire using a battery and steel wool, but with patience and persistence, you should be able to do it. The answer is yes.

Know how to make a fire using a chemical

Starting a fire with chemicals is generally not safe because many chemicals can be flammable or explosive, and starting a fire with chemicals can also produce hazardous gases. When starting a fire, it is advisable to utilize a safer approach, such as matches or a lighter.

If you must use a chemical to ignite a fire, use caution and carefully follow any directions that come with the chemical. Some chemicals, such as calcium carbide, can be used to generate a small spark when they come into contact with water; however, these should be handled with caution since they can be harmful.

It is also critical to have a mechanism to extinguish the fire if it becomes out of control, as well as a plan in place in case of an emergency.

In general, it is safer and more successful to ignite a fire with a safer means, such as matches or a lighter.

Find food

Finding food in the wilderness might be a difficult survival skill, but based on your location and the resources available, you have numerous possibilities. Here are some tips for finding food in the forest:

Identify the following food plants: There are various edible plants that can be found in the forest, including berries, nuts, roots, and leaves. You can utilize a field guide or seek the help of an experienced outdoorsperson to identify edible plants. When hunting for plants, only consume plants that you are certain are safe and non-toxic.

Look for animals: Many woodlands are home to a variety of animals that can be caught or trapped for sustenance. Rabbits, squirrels, birds, and fish are all popular choices. If you choose to hunt or trap animals, make sure you do it responsibly and sustainably.

Look for insects. Insects can be a source of protein in the forest. Beetles, grasshoppers, ants, and worms are all edible insects. You can catch insects with a net, a trap, or your hands. Make sure to eat only non-toxic and harmless insects.

Gather and cook food: Once you've discovered food, you'll need to gather and prepare it for consumption. To transport food, you can use a bag, a basket, or a container. To cook food, you can use a fire, a stove, or other cooking equipment.

Avoid feeding plants or animals with evident evidence of disease or contamination, such as mildew or parasites.

When foraging for food in the wild, keep in mind any allergies or sensitivities you may have.

Handle wild animals with caution, as some may carry diseases or be deadly.

If you can't find any food, look for other sources of nutrition, such as water or dew.

When foraging for food in the wild, remember to always observe local rules and regulations.

Know basic first aid.

The initial treatment of minor injuries or medical situations is referred to as "basic first aid." Here are some fundamental first aid practices that you should be familiar with:

To stop the bleeding, apply direct pressure to the wound with a clean cloth or bandage. Seek medical attention if the bleeding does not stop within a few minutes or if the wound is deep or serious.

Burns: To treat a burn, run cool water over the area for several minutes. Remove any clothing or jewellery from the afflicted area and cover the burn with a clean, dry cloth. Apply no ointments or butter to the burn. If the burn is serious or covers a large region, get medical assistance.

Choking: If someone is choking, try to get them to cough or do the Heimlich manoeuvre to get the object out of their throat. If the person is unable to speak, breathe, or cough, call 911 and, if you are certified, begin CPR.

Fractures: To treat a fracture, use a splint or a sling to immobilize the injured limb. Do not attempt to realign or push the bone back into position. As quickly as possible, get medical assistance.

Shock is a medical emergency that arises when the body does not receive adequate blood flow. Lay the sufferer down with their feet raised and cover them with a blanket to cure shock. Maintain the person's calm and reassurance. Give the individual nothing to eat or drink. As quickly as possible, get medical assistance. To limit the risk of infection, always wash your hands before and after delivering first aid.

In case of an emergency, always keep a first aid kit on hand. Bandages, gauze, antiseptic wipes, adhesive tape, and over-the-counter pain medicine should all be included in a basic first aid kit.

Check for evidence of respiration and a pulse if you are delivering first aid to someone who is unconscious. If the victim isn't breathing, start CPR if you're certified.

If you are administering first aid to someone who is in extreme pain, attempt to keep them as comfortable as possible. You can help them feel better by using pain medication or other tactics like distraction or relaxation.

If you are giving first aid to someone who has a serious injury or medical condition, seek medical assistance immediately. The sooner the individual receives the correct therapy, the higher his or her prospects of recovery.

Know how to navigate

The process of determining your location and finding your way from one area to another is known as navigation. Here are some fundamental concepts to understand to help you traverse the wilderness:

Use a map and a compass: A map is a graphical depiction of a geographic location that depicts characteristics such as rivers, mountains, and roads. A compass is an instrument that employs a magnetized needle to show magnetic north. To navigate with a map and a compass, you must first align the map with magnetic north by orienting it to the environment around you.

Use landmarks: landmarks are natural or man-made features that can be used to aid with orientation and navigation. Mountains, rivers, roads, and buildings are examples of landmarks.

Follow a bearing: A bearing is a direction measured in degrees. To follow a bearing, you must first align your compass with the desired direction and then walk in that direction.

Use the sun and stars: You can use the sun and stars to help you establish your direction. To utilize the sun as a guide, locate the sun's position in the sky and use it to orient yourself. To utilize the stars as a guide, seek for the North Star (also known as

Polaris), which is visible in the northern hemisphere and is positioned near the North Pole.

It is critical to plan your route ahead of time to avoid potential hazards and make the best use of your time and resources.

When navigating in the outdoors, always take a map and a compass, as well as backup navigation gear, such as a GPS device or a personal locator beacon.

As you explore, be aware of your surroundings and seek for indicators that can help you orient yourself, such as animal trails, changes in flora, or variations in topography.

Stay cool and try to retrace your steps if you feel disoriented or lost. If you can't find your way back, locate a safe spot to stay and wait for help.

Practice navigating in various places and conditions to help you improve your skills and get more comfortable with the process.

Know how to signal for help.

If you are lost in the woods and require assistance, there are various ways to signal for help:

Make use of a signalling device: A signalling device is a tool that can be used to draw rescuers' attention. A mirror, a whistle, or a torch are examples of signalling devices. Hold a signalling device up and move it in a way that will attract the attention of rescuers, such as flashing it or making a loud noise.

Build a signal fire. A signal fire is a fire that is built specifically to attract the attention of rescuers. To build a signal fire, gather dry, flammable materials and build a fire in a clearing or other open area. Make the fire as large as possible and keep it burning until rescuers arrive.

Leave a trail: If you are unable to stay in one spot, you can try to leave a trail to help rescuers follow your path. You can leave a trail by using paint, ribbon, or other materials to mark trees or other items.

Use a signalling code: A signalling code is a set of signals used to communicate with rescuers. The international distress signal (three whistle blasts or three light flashes), the SOS signal (three dots followed by three dashes followed by three dots), and the Mayday signal are all examples of signalling codes (the word "Mayday" spoken three times).

Know how to handle wild animals.

If you are in the forest and encounter a wild animal, it is vital to remember that wild animals can be unpredictable and even deadly. Here are some suggestions for dealing with the situation:

Maintain your cool and avoid making unexpected movements. Wild animals are more likely to attack if they feel threatened or surprised.

Avoid approaching the animal. Give the animal lots of space and avoid touching or feeding it.

If the animal is acting aggressively, try raising your arms or expanding your coat to make yourself appear larger.

If the animal attacks, use any weapons you have available to defend yourself, such as a walking stick or a bear horn.

If the animal is not attacking but you feel threatened, attempt to back away from it slowly and gently. Turning your back on the animal or fleeing may set off the animal's predatory instincts.

It's also a good idea to be familiar with the types of wild creatures that live in the area you're visiting and to take necessary measures, such as bringing bear spray if you're in bear country.

Make noise to alert the animal to your presence. This can help the animal avoid an accidental encounter with you.

Pets should be kept on a leash and under supervision. Pets may be viewed as prey by wild animals, and they may attack if they feel threatened.

Pay attention to any signs or warnings regarding wild animals in the area. These are frequently placed in place for your safety, and it is critical that you observe them.

Avoid camping or trekking alone in regions known to have wild animals. In the event of an emergency, it is always a good idea to have a buddy with you.

If you come into contact with a wild animal and cannot safely retreat, try to keep as still as possible and avoid establishing eye contact with the animal. This can help defuse the situation, and the animal may lose interest and move on.

Know how to deal with hypothermia and frostbite.

When a person is exposed to cold temperatures for an extended period, two significant medical disorders can occur: hypothermia and frostbite. Here are some suggestions for dealing with these conditions:

Hypothermia:

Remove the person as quickly as possible from the cold surroundings.

If the person is damp, remove any wet clothing and wrap them in a dry blanket or warm clothing.

Give the person warm liquids, such as water or broth, to drink. Give them no alcohol or caffeine.

Do not give the person anything to drink if they are unconscious or have difficulty swallowing.

As quickly as possible, get medical assistance.

Cover the person's head and neck with a warm hat or scarf to help conserve body heat.

Encourage the individual to move around if they are able to do so in order to raise their body temperature.

If the person is unconscious or unable to walk, place them on their back with their feet slightly elevated.

Do not administer direct heat, such as from a heating pad or hot water bottle, to the person's skin. This can cause burns.

Maintain the person's warmth and comfort until medical assistance comes.

Frostbite:

Remove the person as quickly as possible from the cold surroundings.

Warm water should be used to gently warm the frostbitten parts (about 104–108 degrees Fahrenheit). Use of hot water or a heating pad might result in burns.

Avoid rubbing or massaging the frostbitten regions.

Do not allow the frostbitten regions to get frozen again.

As quickly as possible, get medical assistance.

Breaking blisters or removing frozen tissue should be avoided. This can result in additional damage and an increased risk of infection.

Protect the frostbitten areas from further harm by covering them with a sterile bandage or clean cloth.

Do not try to separate the person's frostbitten fingers or toes if they are stuck together.

To warm frostbitten areas, do not use a heating pad or hot water bottle.

Keep the frostbitten areas elevated to aid in the reduction of enema.

When dealing with hypothermia or frostbite, it is critical to act fast because these symptoms are dangerous and can cause irreversible harm if not treated rapidly. If you believe that someone is suffering from hypothermia or frostbite, get medical attention as quickly as possible.

Know how to deal with heat stroke and dehydration.

Heat stroke and dehydration are two medical diseases that can develop when a person is exposed to excessive heat or does not drink enough fluids. Here are some suggestions for dealing with these conditions:

Heat stroke:

Immediately summon medical assistance. Heat stroke is a dangerous ailment that can be fatal.

Move the person to a cool, shaded area.

Help the person remove superfluous garments.

Fan the person and apply cool, wet clothes or towels to the skin.

Give the person short sips of cool water if they are conscious and able to swallow. Give them no alcohol or caffeine.

Monitor the person's vital signs, such as their pulse and breathing.

Apply ice packs or cold compresses to the individual's neck, armpits, and groin. These places have a lot of blood vessels close to the skin's surface, which might help cool the blood and body faster.

Cool the person's skin with a misting spray or a hand-held fan.

Unless told otherwise by a medical practitioner, do not administer any medications to the individual.

If the person is vomiting or unable to swallow, do not give them any fluids.

Keep the sufferer lying down and slightly elevate their feet to help increase circulation.

Dehydration:

Hydrate yourself with water or sports drinks. The term "electronic commerce" refers to the sale of electronic goods.

Consume foods high in water content, such as fruits and vegetables.

In hot or humid weather, avoid intense activities.

Wear light, loose clothing and a cap to stay cool.

If possible, stay in an air-conditioned environment.

Seek medical attention if your symptoms persist or become severe.

Fluids should be consumed slowly and in small amounts. This can aid in the absorption of fluids by your body.

Avoid drinking significant amounts of fluids at once, as this might cause dehydration.

Drink electrolyte-containing fluids, such as sports drinks or coconut water. These can help your body retain fluids and replace lost minerals.

If you're vomiting or have diarrhoea, use an oral rehydration solution like Pedialyte to restore lost fluids and electrolytes.

Seek medical treatment if you are unable to swallow fluids or are having severe symptoms.

Both heat stroke and dehydration can be serious diseases, especially in young children, elderly adults, and people with underlying medical issues. If you or someone you are with is having severe symptoms, seek medical attention as soon as possible.

Know how to use basic tools:

In the forest, basic tools can be handy for several tasks like shelter construction, fire starting, and food preparation. Here are some pointers on how to use some typical forest tools:

Knife: A knife can be used for many things, including cutting rope, carving wood, and cooking meals. When using a knife, be sure to handle it gently and keep the blade away from your body.

Axe: An axe can be used to chop wood for a fire or to construct a shelter. To avoid injury when wielding an axe, make sure to practice good technique. Stand with your feet shoulder-width apart and both hands on the handle. Swing the axe in a smooth, controlled motion, utilizing your body weight to assist in power generation.

Saw: A saw can be used to cut through wood or other materials. When using a saw, hold the handle with one hand and place the blade against the material you want to cut. Pull the saw back and forth in a steady, smooth manner.

Shovel: A shovel is useful for excavating holes and cleaning debris. Grip the handle with both hands and push down on the top of the handle to drive the blade into the ground when using a shovel.

A multitool is a small tool that contains several instruments, such as a knife, pliers, and screwdrivers. Multitools can be useful for things such as gear repair and minor repairs.

It is crucial to handle all tools with care and follow adequate safety standards to avoid injury. If you are unfamiliar with a tool, be sure to read the instructions or get help from someone who is knowledgeable in its use.

Know how to use a survival kit:

A survival kit is a collection of materials that can assist you in an emergency, such as becoming lost in the woods or stranded in your automobile during a winter storm. Here are some pointers on how to use a survival kit:

Before you need to utilize your survival kit, familiarize yourself with its contents. This will help you understand what tools and services are available to you in the event of a crisis.

Prioritize your needs. Your first concern in a survival situation should be handling any immediate hazards to your safety, such as hypothermia, thirst, or injury.

Use the supplies in your survival kit wisely. For example, use your knife or multi-tool to cut materials for a shelter or to make a fire and your signalling device to summon assistance if necessary.

Always keep your survival gear with you, especially when you are in a wilderness or remote region.

Be willing to improvise. Because you may not always have the precise item you require, it is critical to think creatively and use what you do have to satisfy your needs.

Maintain your cool and keep your head clear. Panic can lead to poor decision-making, so try to stay focused and thoroughly analyse your options.

Understand your limitations. If you haven't been educated in wilderness survival, it's critical to realize when you're in over your head and seek assistance from qualified professionals or local authorities.

Practice good hygiene. In a survival situation, excellent cleanliness can help keep you healthy and happy. To keep yourself clean, use wet wipes, hand sanitizer, and toothpaste.

Keep warm and dry. Staying warm and dry in frigid weather can be a matter of life and death. Thermal blankets and hand warmers can help you regulate your body temperature, and a tarp or emergency blanket can be used to form a makeshift shelter if necessary.

Keep hydrated. Dehydration can be a severe issue in a survival situation, so it's crucial to have a technique to filter water and to take enough water with you to meet your needs. If you can't find a clean water source, use water purification tablets or a portable water filter.

Remember, the key to using a survival kit is to stay calm, think creatively, and use your resources wisely. Always be prepared for the possibility of an emergency, and make sure you have the skills and knowledge you need to stay safe in any situation.

Know how to use a satellite phone or personal locator beacon:

If you are in a forest and need to use a satellite phone or personal locator beacon (PLB), here are some measures you can follow:

Locate a clear spot with a clear view of the sky. Satellite phones and PLBs rely on a clear line of sight to the satellite to function, so locate a location where you can see as much of the sky as possible.

To use the gadget, follow the manufacturer's instructions. Because each satellite phone and PLB is unique, it is critical to carefully read and follow the instructions.

If you are using a satellite phone, call for help. Dial the proper emergency number for your location (for example, 911 in the United States) and describe your issue thoroughly. If you are using a PLB, activate the beacon according to the manufacturer's instructions.

Stay put and wait for aid to arrive. It's crucial to stay in one spot and not try to wander around in search of aid, as this can make it harder for rescue personnel to discover you. Maintain your warmth, dryness, and hydration, and use your survival gear to meet your basic needs until aid arrives.

Make a strategy. Take a minute to analyse your position and consider what you need to do to stay safe before using your satellite phone or PLB. Consider your surroundings, the weather, and any injuries or medical concerns you may have.

signal for aid. If you don't have a satellite phone or PLB, consider signalling for assistance through other means. This could include constructing a signal fire, using a whistle or other signalling device, or placing a brightly coloured piece of clothing in a visible area.

Collect resources. While you wait for assistance, try to collect any supplies that may be valuable to you, such as firewood, food, water, and shelter materials.

Keep warm and dry. It is critical to stay warm and dry in cold weather to avoid hypothermia. Make a shelter out of things from your survival kit and attempt to keep your body temperature up by being active and drinking warm drinks.

Maintain your health. In a survival situation, it's crucial to take care of your bodily and emotional health. Stay hydrated, eat whenever possible, and get plenty of rest. If you have any injuries or medical conditions, do everything you can to treat them and keep them from worsening.

Remember that satellite phones and PLBs are only to be utilized in life-threatening situations. If you become lost in the woods and don't have a satellite phone or a personal locator beacon, try to stay cool and use basic survival methods like locating a shelter, signalling for aid, and staying hydrated.

Know how to improvise

If you become lost in the woods, it is crucial to remain calm and think logically in order to find your way out or to live until help arrives. Here are some strategies for improvising in a survival situation:

Examine your circumstances. Take a few moments to assess your surroundings and see what resources are accessible to you. Consider your surroundings, the weather, and any injuries or medical concerns you may have.

Seek refuge. Look for natural protection, such as a cave or overhang, or craft a makeshift shelter out of materials found in your surroundings. If you have a tarp or an emergency blanket, make a small building to protect yourself from the elements.

Collect resources. Look for food, water, and other resources that will allow you to meet your basic needs. Berries, nuts, and other food plants may be included, as well as fresh water supplies such as streams or lakes.

signal for aid. If you think rescue is conceivable, try to signal for help using any means accessible to you. This could include constructing a signal fire, using a whistle or other signalling device, or placing a brightly coloured piece of clothing in a visible area.

Keep warm and dry. It is critical to stay warm and dry in cold weather to avoid hypothermia. Use natural things to insulate yourself, such as leaves and branches, and attempt to keep your body temperature up by being active and drinking warm drinks.

Remember that staying calm, thinking creatively, and using your resources properly are the keys to improvising in a survival crisis. Always be ready for an emergency and ensure you have the skills and knowledge you need to keep safe in any situation.

Know how to purify water using chemicals or a water filter.

There are numerous ways to purify water using chemicals or a water filter, depending on the resources you have available. Here are some methods for purifying water in a survival situation:

Locate a water source. Look for water sources such as streams, lakes, or rivers. Avoid drinking water that is obviously dirty or contaminated, as well as water with a strong, disagreeable smell.

Gather the water. Collect the water in a clean container or water bottle. If you don't have a container, you can catch and hold the water with a piece of clothing or a huge leaf.

Water should be pre-treated. Allow any sediment to settle to the bottom for a while if the water is hazy or muddy. To remove any visible debris, strain the water through a piece of cloth or a coffee filter.

To purify the water, use chemicals. If you have water purification pills or liquid bleach, you can use these chemicals to purify the water. Follow the manufacturer's directions for how much to use and how long to wait before drinking the water.

Use a water filter. You can purify the water with a water filter, such as a straw filter or a gravity filter.

Follow the manufacturer's recommendations for cleaning and maintaining the filter.

Make use of a solar still. If you don't have access to chemicals or a water filter, you can purify water with a solar still. A solar still is a simple apparatus that evaporates and condenses water from a polluted source using the heat of the sun.

The term "electronic commerce" refers to the sale of electronic goods. A LifeStraw is a compact, portable water filter that you can use to drink directly from a water source. Suck the water through the filter by inserting the straw into the water.

Use a water bottle with an integrated filter. Many water bottles now come with built-in filters that can remove pollutants from the water as you drink it. Simply fill the bottle with water and sip through the filter as you would normally.

Use a ceramic filter. A ceramic filter is a type of water filter that removes pollutants from water by using a porous ceramic substance. These filters can eliminate germs, viruses, and other pollutants, but they are time-consuming to use and may necessitate frequent cleaning.

Make use of a UV water purifier. A UV water purifier is a device that kills bacteria, viruses, and other pollutants in water by using ultraviolet radiation. These devices are portable and simple to use, but they do require an electrical source to function.

Remember to carefully purify the water to verify that it is safe to drink. If you're in a survival situation and don't have chemicals or a water filter, you can purify water by boiling it for at least one minute. This will eliminate any potentially hazardous bacteria and parasites.

Know how to find and use edible plants

Look for plants that have recognizable traits. If you are unfamiliar with the local flora, seek out plants that have similar traits to plants you already know are edible. Look for plants with thistles, thorns, or lobed leaves, as these are common signs of edible plants.

Identify edible plants using your senses. You can recognize edible plants by using your senses of sight, smell, and touch. Look for plants with brightly coloured berries or blooms, as well as leaves with a pleasing scent. You can also touch the plant to determine if it feels smooth or rough, or if it has any strange textures.

Avoid plants that have toxic properties. Some plants have harmful properties that can assist you in identifying them as inedible. White berries, milky sap, or a harsh or caustic flavour are examples. If you come across a plant that exhibits any of these traits, it's advisable to avoid it.

Use the "Universal Edibility Test" if you are unsure. If you are unsure whether a plant is safe to eat, you can use the "Universal Edibility Test" to help you decide. This test entails biting a little piece of the plant, holding it in your mouth for 15 minutes, and then spitting it out. If you have no adverse effects, try a small bite of the plant to see if it causes stomach upset.

The term "electronic commerce" refers to the sale of electronic goods. You can use a plant identification guide or app to help you identify the plants in your region if you have access to one. These resources can provide knowledge on the properties, applications, and edibility of certain plants, which can be useful in a survival situation.

Remember, it's crucial to be cautious while using edible plants in a survival situation. If you are unsure whether a plant is safe to consume, avoid it. Always be ready for an emergency and ensure you have the skills and knowledge you need to keep safe in any situation.

Know how to set traps and snares:

Here are some measures you can take if you find yourself in a survival crisis in the wilderness and need to set traps and snares to collect food:

Choose an appropriate place for your traps and snares. Look for places where animals are known to congregate, such as paths, drinking holes, or food supplies.

The term "electronic commerce" refers to the sale of electronic goods. Look for vines, twigs, and branches to utilize as bait or to make the structure of your traps. Avoid using synthetic materials, as these might shatter or become damaged easily.

To attract animals, use bait. You can use bait such as berries, nuts, or other food items to draw animals to your traps and snares. Make sure the bait is visible and easy for the animals to get.

Make simple but efficient traps and snares. There are many different types of traps and snares you can design, but it's crucial to make them basic and effective. Small animals can be caught with a simple snare built from a bent sapling and a cordage noose.

Check your traps and snares on a regular basis. It is critical to check your traps and snares on a frequent basis to see whether anything has been caught and to reset them if required. Prepare to change your traps and snares as needed depending on the species you're after and the conditions in your area.

To disguise your traps and snares, use natural camouflage. Animals are more likely to fall for your traps if they cannot see or smell them; thus, it is critical to disguise your traps and snares with natural camouflage. You can hide and mix in your traps with branches, leaves, and other natural materials.

To activate your traps and snares, use trigger mechanisms. When an animal takes the bait, the trigger mechanism initiates the trap or snare. You can employ a variety of trigger devices, such as a simple peg or stick that holds the trap open until the animal disturbs it.

For different animals, use different types of traps and snares. Because different animals have varied habits and behaviours, it's critical to select the appropriate type of trap or snare for the species you're after. A deadfall trap, for example, may be useful for catching small mammals, whereas a fish trap may be more effective for catching fish.

Use a variety of traps and snares. You can boost your chances of catching food by setting many traps and snares in different areas. This will also allow you to target a wide range of animals.

Remember, it's important to be respectful of the animals you are trapping and to use traps and snares only as a last resort in a survival situation. Always be prepared for the possibility of an emergency, and make sure you have the skills and knowledge you need to stay safe in any situation.

Know how to fish.

Seek out bodies of water like streams, rivers, or lakes. These are expected to include a diverse range of fish species.

Look for fish indications, such as ripples on the water's surface or birds diving into the water to capture fish.

Make a fishing line and hook out of natural materials. Plants, vines, or even your own hair can be used.

To attract fish, use bait. Insects, worms, and small parts of edible plants or animals can all be used.

To catch fish, try using a homemade spear or harpoon. Sharpening the end of a stick or utilizing a sharpened pebble can be used to make a spear.

Consider making a basic fish trap by erecting a barrier across a stream or river or catching fish in a basket or container.

Look for additional sources of food, such as berries, nuts, and edible plants, as well as tiny animals that can be caught and eaten.

Keep a watch out for predators like bears and other large animals and take precautions if required.

Drink pure water from streams or lakes to stay hydrated.

If you become lost in the forest and lack the essential skills or expertise to catch fish, it is critical to prioritize your safety and attempt to return to society as quickly as possible.

Know how to make a spear.

If you become lost in the woods and need to build a spear, you can do so by following these steps:

Find a long, straight branch that can support the weight of whatever you intend to spear. The branch should be around the thickness of your thumb and the length of your arm.

Sharpen the branch's one end with a rock or other sharp item. You can accomplish this by carefully scraping the branch's end on the rock until it becomes pointed.

Find a flexible vine or piece of bark and secure it around the base of the sharpened branch end. This will help hold the spearhead in place.

Locate a good material for a spearhead. This could be a sharpened piece of bone, a sharpened rock, or a piece of flint. Using the vine or bark, secure the spearhead to the sharpened end of the branch.

Holding the spear in your hand and feeling how it feels will help you determine its balance. If the spearhead is too heavy or the handle is too light, the balance may need to be adjusted by adding or subtracting weight from one end or the other.

Practice using the spear to obtain a sense of its balance and movement. To practice, throw sticks or other small items into the air and try to spear them, or simply move the spear around and get a feel for how it handles. This will assist you in becoming more comfortable and proficient with utilizing the spear, which could be vital if you need to rely on it for hunting or self-defence. It is vital to remember that using a spear for hunting or self-defence is risky and should only be done in an emergency. If you become lost in the woods, your first goal should be to find a means to return to civilization or to your home.

Know how to make a bow and arrows.

Choose an appropriate piece of wood for the bow. This should be a long, straight branch that can bend and retain its shape. The wood should be sturdy and largely free of knots and other flaws.

Bend the wood into a "C" shape and secure it with a flexible vine or bark to create a bow shape. You can make this by tying the vine or bark around the centre of the bow and then drawing the ends in opposite directions to form it.

Choose an appropriate material for the bowstrings. A strong vine, a piece of sinew, or even a thin strip of bark might be used. Tie the bowstrings to the bow's ends with a knot or tie them in place.

Choose a suitable substance for the arrows. Straight and knot-free thin branches or reeds could be used. The arrows must be trimmed or shaved to a uniform size and shape.

Sharpen one end of each arrow using a rock or other sharp item. This is the point from which you will hunt or protect yourself.

Find an appropriate material to utilize as fletching for the arrows. This could be feathers, leaves, or even thin strips of bark. Using a flexible vine or bark, attach the fletching to the back end of each arrow.

Get a sense for how the bow and arrows work by practicing with them. This can be accomplished by firing at targets or simply acquiring a feel for how the bowstring feels when drawn back and released.

It is vital to note that using a bow and arrows for hunting or self-defence can be dangerous and should only be done in a survival emergency. If you become lost in the woods, your first goal should be to find a path back to civilization or to seek assistance.

What not to do if you want to survive in the forest

There are things you should avoid doing if you wish to survive in the forest:

Don't freak out; keep a clear head and be calm. This will assist you in thinking clearly and making sound decisions.

Stay close to your campsite: If you become lost, being close to your campsite will make it simpler for search and rescue workers to find you.

Drink only purified water. River, lake, and stream water may contain germs and parasites that can make you sick. Boil or purify the water before drinking it.

Do not rely on a single food source. Relying on a single food source can lead to malnutrition. Find a range of food sources, such as berries, nuts, and small animals.

Avoid being out in the elements by seeking shelter from the rain, wind, and sun. Wear layers of clothing to remain warm and use natural resources like leaves and branches to form a makeshift shelter.

Don't rely solely on the light of the sun to navigate: the sun, especially when it's foggy, can be deceiving. Use a map and compass, or other navigational tools, to locate your way.

Don't use your phone or other electronics: These devices can quickly deplete your battery, and they may not operate if you are in a remote place without cell phone coverage.

Don't build a fire in a risky location. Build a fire only in a specified fire pit or in a safe area away from combustible things.

Don't squander energy; only engage in tasks that are vital for survival.

Don't disregard your essential needs: make sure to drink enough water, eat frequently, and get enough rest.

Don't presume you know it all. Keep an open mind to new survival tactics and approaches and be willing to adapt to your surroundings. You can improve your chances of survival in the jungle by following these guidelines. It's also a good idea to be prepared before venturing out into the woods by packing the essential supplies and learning some survival techniques.